BEGINNING HISTORY

NORMAN CASTLES

Graham Rickard

Illustrated by Michael Bragg

BEGINNING HISTORY

Crusaders
Egyptian Pyramids
Greek Cities
Medieval Markets
Norman Castles
Roman Soldiers
Saxon Villages
Tudor Sailors
Victorian Children
Viking Explorers

All words that appear in **bold** are explained in the glossary on page 22

Series editor: Catherine Ellis
Book editor: Rosemary Ashley

First published in 1989 by Wayland (Publishers) Limited
61 Western Road, Hove, East Sussex, BN3 1KD

British Library Cataloguing in Publication Data
Rickard, Graham
Norman castles
1. England castles, history
I. Title
942

ISBN 1–85210–774–X

Typeset by Kalligraphics Limited, Horley, Surrey
Printed in Italy by G. Canale & C.S.p.A.
Bound in Belgium by Casterman S.A.

CONTENTS

WHO WERE THE NORMANS?

The word Norman means man from the north. The first Norman people were Viking warriors from **Scandinavia**, who **invaded** an area of Northern France which is now called Normandy.

The Normans had a **feudal** system of government, which meant that everyone served their local lord or **baron** in return for strips of land on which they could grow food. In the same way, all the lords served their king in return for having control over their own area. The Normans were very good soldiers, and Norman **knights** wore metal **armour** and rode horses when fighting their enemies.

A Norman lord surveys his lands as he returns to his castle from a hunting trip.

The barons built strong castles to defend themselves, and these castles soon became important centres of feudal society. The Norman castle was the baron's home and fortress. It was also bank, prison, police station, tax office, and law court for the area which he controlled.

A scene from the Bayeux Tapestry of Norman knights galloping into battle.

5

Norman Invaders

After settling in northern France, the Normans began to invade other parts of Europe, and soon had control of Sicily and southern Italy.

In the year 1066, the Norman king, William the Conqueror, decided to invade England. He gathered his army on the French coast and sailed across the Channel to claim the English throne. The English **Saxon** king Harold marched his army south to stop the Norman invaders, and the two armies met at the Battle of

Above *A foot soldier in full armour and carrying his weapons and shield.*

Right *The Norman fleet crossing the Channel on their way to invade England.*

6

Hastings, not far from the coast where the Normans had landed. King Harold was killed in the battle, and William was crowned as the new English king.

As the Normans conquered the rest of England, they built hundreds of small wooden castles to protect themselves, and from which they could control the local people.

The coronation of King William I of England, after he defeated King Harold at the Battle of Hastings.

7

WOODEN CASTLES

The first Norman castles were quickly built, to protect the Norman barons and their knights, and to control the local Saxon people. Some early castles were circular banks of earth surrounded by a ditch. Others, called motte and bailey castles, had a square wooden fort or **keep** built on top of a mound of earth, called the **motte**. The keep was surrounded by a fence of sharp wooden stakes. It was the safest part of the castle. At the foot of the motte was a circular courtyard inside another wooden fence; this was called the **bailey**.

The Normans building their first castle at Hastings. On the left two are fighting a mock battle.

The bailey contained kitchen, stables, bakery and chapel. Outside the fence was a deep ditch, sometimes filled with water, which could only be crossed over a **drawbridge**. The drawbridge was raised if the castle was attacked.

These wooden castles could be easily burned, or smashed with **battering rams**, and many were soon replaced with stronger stone castles.

A Saxon tribe makes a surprise attack on a Norman castle, and sets fire to the wooden buildings.

STONE CASTLES

This strong stone castle at Rochester in Kent has walls which are 3.6 m thick.

The Normans built castles in large towns, along borders, and to protect important river crossings and roads. They replaced their wooden castles with stone ones, which were much stronger. The Tower of London is the most famous of the Normans' stone castles, but there are many others which still survive. These castles have thick outer walls, with towers and gaps at the top called **battlements**, from which **archers** fired their arrows. Inside the walls a strong stone keep was built.

On the ground floor of the keep was a storeroom for weapons and armour. Above was the main hall, where the lord and his lady entertained guests and ate their meals. They slept in the top room of the keep, called a **solar**. Most castles had a chapel. Some even had a toilet called a **garderobe**. This was just a hole in the castle walls.

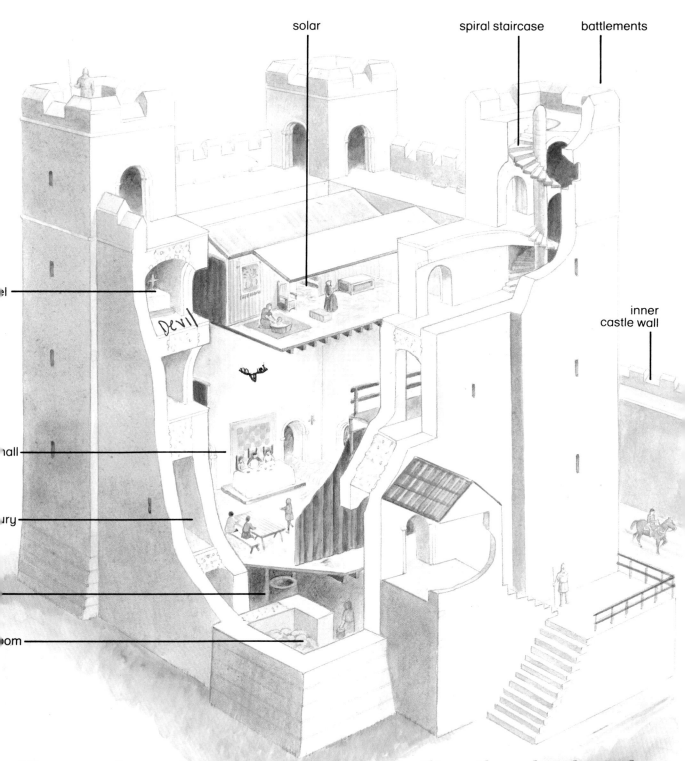

The stone keep of a Norman castle was built on three levels, and the thick outer walls had passages and stairways inside them.

11

BUILDING CASTLES

Building a castle was very hard work and required a large number of skilled people.

Building a stone castle was an enormous task. There was very little machinery and the castle took thousands of men several years to complete. Castles were very expensive to build, and each one cost many millions of pounds in today's prices.

A castle had to be built where there was plenty of food, water, stone and timber. Huge amounts of materials had to be carried to the site, and the local people were often forced to help build the castle.

Stonemasons used ropes and simple cranes to lift the heavy stones into position to build the thick, high walls. Many **carpenters, blacksmiths** and other workers also used their skills to make the floors, doors, chains and furniture which were needed in the castle. Some castles were painted white on the outside, and could be seen from a long way away.

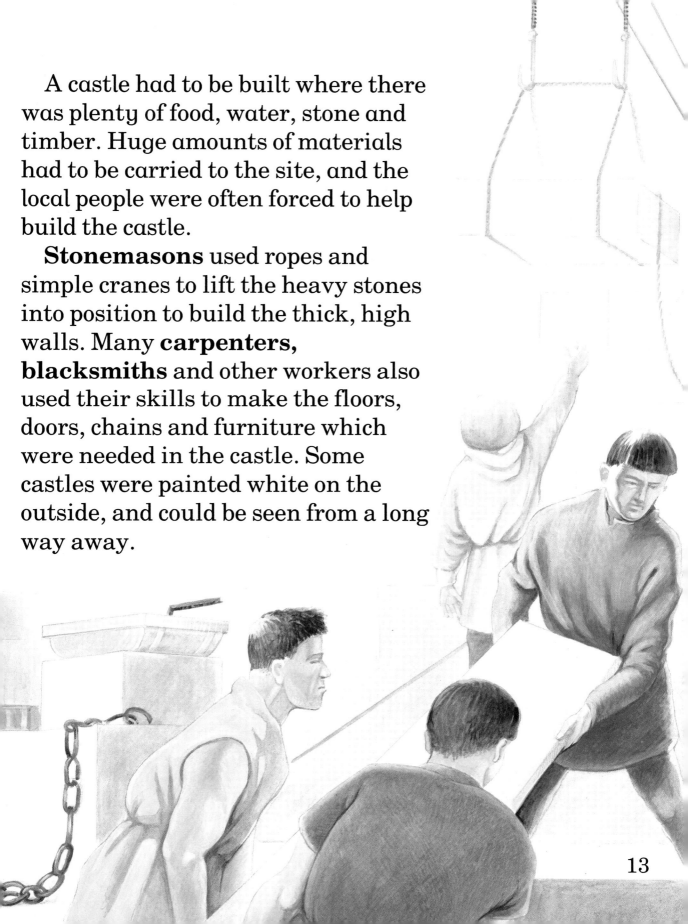

ATTACKING AND DEFENDING A CASTLE

Soldiers attack a castle using a huge catapault to hurl rocks over the walls. The defenders fire arrows and pour down boiling water.

Castles were very difficult to attack. Archers fired their arrows from the battlements, and the entrance to the castle was often guarded by a drawbridge and gatehouse. The gatehouse had a metal gate, called a **portcullis**, which was lowered in times of attack. Inside the gatehouse, attackers faced a hail of arrows fired from slits in the side walls, and large stones, or boiling water dropped from the roof.

Attacking armies might use ladders to climb the castle walls, or try to smash the gates and walls with battering rams. Or they might tunnel beneath the walls and light a fire to make them collapse. They also used huge **catapults**, to fire rocks and burning spears over the walls.

A long **siege** was the commonest form of attack, and sometimes lasted many months. The attackers stopped all supplies from entering the castle, and the people inside had to surrender or starve to death.

PEOPLE IN A CASTLE

Above *Coins from the reign of King William I.*

Below *The armourer checks the blade of a sword while a kitchenmaid pours beer and a boy carries bread from the kitchen.*

A Norman castle was both a home and a fortress. As well as the lord and lady, with their family and friends, fifty people or more lived in the castle.

After the baron the most important person in the castle was the **steward**, a knight who was left in charge of the castle when the baron was away. He organized the running of the castle and its lands, and looked after his lord's money.

Other officials looked after the castle's supplies of food, drink and firewood, and many servants were needed to wash and mend clothes, look after the horses, and carry supplies. Cooks, bakers and brewers produced great quantities of food and beer, while the **armourer** made sure that the soldiers had plenty of bows, arrows, swords and armour.

Carpenters and stonemasons kept the castle in good repair. The priest performed his religious duties and also taught the lord's children.

Two Normans sit down to a meal of wine and cheese. Colourful tapestries were hung on the walls to make the room warmer.

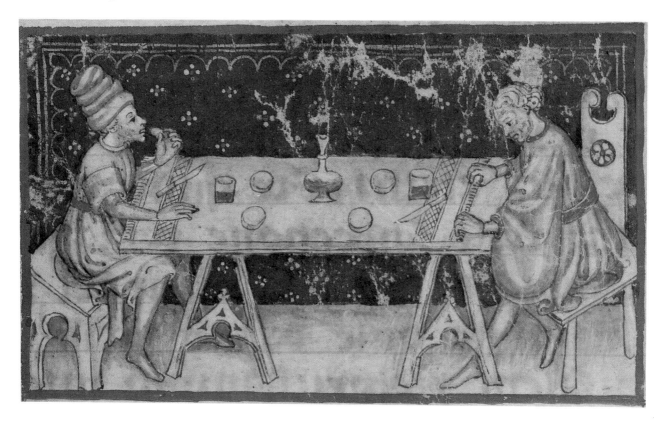

Everyday Life

The castle bailey contained gardens and orchards. Pigs and chickens roamed freely.

Life in a castle was always busy. The lord inspected his lands, and his steward made sure that the farmers paid taxes and provided food for the castle. The lord was also the local judge, and decided what punishments people who had broken the law should be given.

The cooks got up very early, and worked in the bailey to provide food for all the people in the castle. Many people worked in the nearby forests, cutting firewood for the ovens and open fires in the castle.

Most castles had a well to provide water, but it was the **brewer's** job to make the beer which everyone drank with their meals. Gardeners grew vegetables and herbs and kept pigs, cattle and bees inside the castle walls.

In the stables, the grooms looked after the horses. The soldiers sharpened their weapons and practised their archery. They took turns in keeping a watch out for enemies.

In the **forge** the blacksmith made swords, spears and shields, and other weapons, as well as horseshoes and kitchen pots.

A carved ivory ornament showing Normans playing chess.

Castle Amusements

Living in a castle was not all hard work, and there were plenty of things to keep people amused in their spare time. For the lord and his friends, the favourite sport was hunting. They rode on horses, using dogs and **falcons** as well as bows and arrows to hunt deer, wild boar and other animals, which they brought back to the castle to be cooked.

Most people lived, ate and slept together. In the evenings, they ate at large tables in the great hall, using knives and fingers, because they had no forks. Bones and scraps were thrown to the dogs on the floor, which was covered with straw.

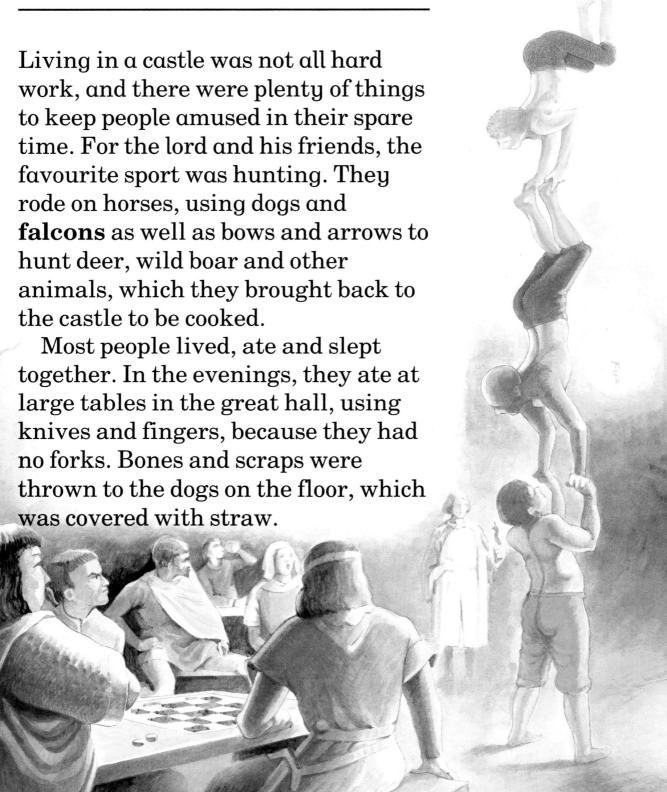

After the meal, people played games such as chess, draughts or dice, and were sometimes entertained by jugglers, musicians and story-tellers.

Occasionally there were exciting entertainments called **tournaments**, when people watched mounted knights in armour pretending to fight.

When the Lord and his lady went upstairs to bed, everyone else wrapped themselves in blankets and lay on the floor to sleep.

Entertainments in the great hall.

GLOSSARY

Archers Men skilled in using bows and arrows as weapons.

Armour Metal protection for soldiers and horses.

Armourer A man who looked after weapons and armour.

Bailey The outer part of a castle.

Baron A Norman lord.

Battering-ram A tree trunk used to knock holes in a castle wall.

Battlements Gaps in the castle walls through which archers fired arrows.

Bayeux Tapestry An 11th century embroidery depicting the Norman invasion of England.

Blacksmith Someone who makes and mends articles of iron.

Brewer A maker of beer.

Carpenter Someone who works with wood.

Catapult A heavy war engine used for hurling stones.

Drawbridge A bridge which can be raised and lowered.

Falcon A kind of bird used for hunting.

Forge A place where the blacksmith works, making things from metal.

Garderobe A simple toilet in a castle.

Invade To enter and occupy a country with military forces.

Keep The strong inner tower of a castle.

Knight A man who served his lord as a mounted and armed soldier.

Motte A mound of earth with a keep on top.

Portcullis A large metal gate which was raised or lowered.

Saxons The people who lived in England before the Normans invaded.

Scandinavia The countries of northern Europe, including Sweden, Norway and Denmark.

Siege An attempt to capture a fortress or town by surrounding it so that those inside will be starved out.

Solar The top room of the keep, used as the lord's bedroom.

Steward Someone who manages an estate.

Stonemason Someone who prepares stone for building.

Tournament An event where knights pretended to fight, or joust.

BOOKS TO READ

A Trip to a Castle by E. Holmes (Nelson, 1974)

Castles by David Woodlander (A. & C. Black Ltd., 1983)

Castles and Mansions by Alan James (Wayland, 1988)

Knights And Castles by D.J.Hall (Arnold, 1975)

Living in a Castle by R.J.Unstead (A. & C. Black, 1971)

See Inside a Castle by R.J.Unstead (Hutchinson, 1977)

The Castle Story by Sheila Sancha (Kestrel Books, 1979)

INDEX

Picture Acknowledgements

The illustrations appearing on the following pages were provided by: Michael Holford 5, 6 (lower), 8, 10; Ronald Sheridan 16, 19; Wayland Picture 6 (top), 17. Artwork on page 11 is by Jenny Hughes.